FRANCIS FRITH'S

HERTFORDSHIRE
REVISITED
PHOTOGRAPHIC
MEMORIES

THE FRANCIS FRITH COLLECTION

www.francisfrith.com

FRANCIS FRITH'S

HERTFORDSHIRE REVISITED

PHOTOGRAPHIC MEMORIES

TOM DOIG is a social historian researching rural life in the 19th and 20th century. He is well known for his books on local history and for his radio and television programmes. During the 1980s he held the post of Director of the Cambridge and County Folk Museum. Tom is currently running a number of lectures for the Workers Education Association based in Cambridge, as well as giving talks to local history, amenity and family history groups. He lives in a remote part of north Hertfordshire in a converted cattle shed built during the 1840s as part of a model farmstead. A qualified teacher and automobile engineer, he is interested in promoting local history and engineering in his local primary school, where he oversees a weekly engineers' club. When relaxing from his history research, Tom devotes his time to the restoration of a vintage-style sports car and helping to run a Cambridgeshire motor racing team.

FRANCIS FRITH'S
PHOTOGRAPHIC MEMORIES

HERTFORDSHIRE REVISITED

PHOTOGRAPHIC MEMORIES

TOM DOIG

First published in the United Kingdom in 2011 by
The Francis Frith Collection®

Paperback Edition ISBN 978-1-84589-562-4

British Library Cataloguing in Publication Data

Hertfordshire Revisited Photographic Memories
Tom Doig

The Francis Frith Collection
Unit 6, Oakley Business Park,
Wylye Road, Dinton,
Wiltshire SP3 5EU
Tel: +44 (0) 1722 716 376
Email: info@francisfrith.co.uk
www.francisfrith.com

Printed and bound in England

Front Cover: **ST ALBANS,** *Holywell Hill 1921* 70480t
Frontispiece: **BUNTINGFORD,** *Market Hill 1923* 74923
*The colour-tinting is for illustrative purposes only, and is not intended
to be historically accurate*

CONTENTS

FRANCIS FRITH
VICTORIAN PIONEER

FRANCIS FRITH, founder of the world-famous photographic archive, was a complex and multi-talented man. A devout Quaker and a highly successful Victorian businessman, he was philosophical by nature and pioneering in outlook.

By 1855 he had already established a wholesale grocery business in Liverpool, and sold it for the astonishing sum of £200,000, which is the equivalent today of over £15,000,000. Now a very rich man, he was able to indulge his passion for travel. As a child he had pored over travel books written by early explorers, and his fancy and imagination had been stirred by family holidays to the sublime mountain regions of Wales and Scotland. 'What lands of spirit-stirring and enriching scenes and places!' he had written. He was to return to these scenes of grandeur in later years to 'recapture the thousands of vivid and tender memories', but with a different purpose. Now in his thirties, and captivated by the new science of photography, Frith set out on a series of pioneering journeys up the Nile and to the Near East that occupied him from 1856 until 1860.

INTRIGUE AND EXPLORATION

These far-flung journeys were packed with intrigue and adventure. In his life story, written when he was sixty-three, Frith tells of being held captive by bandits, and of fighting 'an awful midnight battle to the very point of surrender with a deadly pack of hungry, wild dogs'. Wearing flowing Arab costume, Frith arrived at Akaba by camel sixty years before Lawrence of Arabia, where he encountered 'desert princes and rival sheikhs, blazing with jewel-hilted swords'.

He was the first photographer to venture beyond the sixth cataract of the Nile. Africa was still the mysterious 'Dark Continent', and Stanley and Livingstone's historic meeting was a decade into the future. The conditions for picture taking confound belief. He laboured for hours in his wicker dark-room in the sweltering heat of the desert, while the volatile chemicals fizzed dangerously in their trays. Back in London he exhibited his photographs and was 'rapturously cheered' by members of the Royal Society. His reputation as a photographer was made overnight.

VENTURE OF A LIFE-TIME

Characteristically, Frith quickly spotted the opportunity to create a new business as a specialist publisher of photographs. He lived in an era of immense and sometimes violent change.

For the poor in the early part of Victoria's reign work was exhausting and the hours long, and people had precious little free time to enjoy themselves. Most had no transport other than a cart or gig at their disposal, and rarely travelled far beyond the boundaries of their own town or village. However, by the 1870s the railways had threaded their way across the country, and Bank Holidays and half-day Saturdays had been made obligatory by Act of Parliament. All of a sudden the working man and his family were able to enjoy days out and see a little more of the world.

With typical business acumen, Francis Frith foresaw that these new tourists would enjoy having souvenirs to commemorate their days out. In 1860 he married Mary Ann Rosling and set out on a new career: his aim was to photograph every city, town and village in Britain. For the next thirty years he travelled the country by train and by pony and trap, producing fine photographs of seaside resorts and beauty spots that were keenly bought by millions of Victorians. These prints were painstakingly pasted into family albums and pored over during the dark nights of winter, rekindling precious memories of summer excursions.

THE RISE OF FRITH & CO

Frith's studio was soon supplying retail shops all over the country. To meet the demand he gathered about him a small team of photographers, and published the work of independent artist-photographers of the calibre of Roger Fenton and Francis Bedford. In order to gain some understanding of the scale of Frith's business one only has to look at the catalogue issued by Frith & Co in 1886: it runs to some 670 pages, listing not only many thousands of views of the British Isles but also many photographs of most European countries, and China, Japan, the USA and Canada - note the sample page shown on page 9 from the hand-written Frith & Co ledgers recording the pictures. By 1890 Frith had created the greatest specialist photographic publishing company in the world, with over 2,000 sales outlets - more than the combined number that Boots and WH Smith have today! The picture on the next page shows the Frith & Co display board at Ingleton in the Yorkshire Dales (left of window). Beautifully constructed with a mahogany frame and gilt inserts, it could display up to a dozen local scenes.

POSTCARD BONANZA

The ever-popular holiday postcard we know today took many years to develop. In 1870 the Post Office issued the first plain cards, with a pre-printed stamp on one face. In 1894 they allowed other publishers' cards to be sent through the mail with an attached adhesive halfpenny stamp. Demand grew rapidly, and in 1895 a new size of postcard was permitted called the court card, but there was little room for illustration. In 1899, a year after Frith's death, a new card measuring 5.5 x 3.5 inches became the standard format, but it was not until 1902 that the divided back came into being, so that the address and message could be on one face and a full-size illustration on the other. Frith & Co were in the vanguard of postcard development: Frith's sons Eustace and Cyril continued their father's monumental task, expanding the number of views offered to the public and recording more and more places in Britain, as the coasts and countryside were opened up to mass travel.

Francis Frith had died in 1898 at his villa in Cannes, his great project still growing. The archive he created continued in business for another seventy years. By 1970 it contained over a third of a million pictures showing 7,000 British towns and villages.

FRANCIS FRITH'S LEGACY

Frith's legacy to us today is of immense significance and value, for the magnificent archive of evocative photographs he created provides a unique record of change in the cities, towns and villages throughout Britain over a century and more. Frith and his fellow studio photographers revisited locations many times down the years to update their views, compiling for us an enthralling and colourful pageant of British life and character.

We are fortunate that Frith was dedicated to recording the minutiae of everyday life, for it is this sheer wealth of visual data, the painstaking chronicle of changes in dress, transport, street layouts, buildings, housing, engineering and landscape that captivates us so much today. His remarkable images offer us a powerful link with the past and with the lives of our ancestors.

THE VALUE OF THE ARCHIVE TODAY

Computers have now made it possible for Frith's many thousands of images to be accessed

almost instantly. Frith's images are increasingly used as visual resources, by social historians, by researchers into genealogy and ancestry, by architects and town planners, and by teachers involved in local history projects.

In addition, the archive offers every one of us an opportunity to examine the places where we and our families have lived and worked down the years. Highly successful in Frith's own era, the archive is now, a century and more on, entering a new phase of popularity. Historians consider the Francis Frith Collection to be of prime national importance. It is the only archive of its kind remaining in private ownership. Francis Frith's archive is now housed in an historic timber barn in the beautiful village of Teffont in Wiltshire. Its founder would not recognize the archive office as it is today. In place of the many thousands of dusty boxes containing glass plate negatives and an all-pervading odour of photographic chemicals, there are now ranks of computer screens. He would be amazed to watch his images travelling round the world at unimaginable speeds through internet lines.

The archive's future is both bright and exciting. Francis Frith, with his unshakeable belief in making photographs available to the greatest number of people, would undoubtedly approve of what is being done today with his lifetime's work. His photographs depicting our shared past are now bringing pleasure and enlightenment to millions around the world a century and more after his death.

HERTFORDSHIRE
AN INTRODUCTION

IF THE CORE of the county of Hertfordshire can be identified in the A1(M) road, then the southern boundary runs close to the line of the M25. The eastern limit follows the line of the River Lea and the New River. There is no historical tradition for the M25, but the A1(M) was the Great North Road, and the River Lea runs parallel to the Roman Ermine Street, now the A10.

Our tour of Hertfordshire is dominated by the theme of transport. An example is the Borough of Broxbourne, an area that was unsure of its identity: Hoddesdon, for instance, was always a disputed part of Great Amwell, located in east Hertfordshire, but the communities of Hoddesdon, Broxbourne, Wormley, Cheshunt and Waltham Cross in the south-eastern side of our county now fall under the benevolent patronage of the Borough of Broxbourne. Like so many urban parts of England, Broxbourne Borough was dismissive about its built and social heritage. But any locality that can boast a massive piece of London's history (Temple Bar), one of the few surviving Eleanor Crosses (Waltham Cross), and a palace used by King James I (Theobalds) has something to shout about. Added to this we have a main Roman arterial road and the home of

John Loudon McAdam, 'the Colossus of Roads', (at Hoddesdon), as well as a large proportion of the 20th century's greatest road building programme - road building is in the blood of the local people.

But it is not only the roads that demonstrated Hertfordshire's recognition of modern engineering - the New River in the 17th century saw the locality at the cutting edge of technology. In the late 1500s, Hugh Myddleton (later Sir Hugh) sought to provide a fresh water supply to the City of London. He identified the pure water springs at Chadwell (close to Great Amwell and south of Ware) as an ideal source, and at his own expense (the corporation of the city refused to contribute!), drove a channel about 40 miles long, via Stoke Newington, to the centre of Clerkenwell. Here hollowed wooden logs served as pipes to distribute the water to the surrounding communities. But the project was not without its difficulties, for part way through the construction work, Myddleton ran out of funds. Had it not been for the timely intervention of the king, the city might have had to continue to rely on its original polluted supply. The New River was opened in 1613 and was formally incorporated as the New River Company in 1619. Though a clean water supply was essential to the survival of the population, it was difficult to garner any revenue from the New River, and it was not until 1631, five years after Myddleton's death, that it returned a profit.

A hundred or so years later, London's demand for water exceeded the supply from Chadwell, and it seemed likely that the spring would be exhausted. Additional water was drawn into the New River from the nearby River Lea through a canal-like cut at King's Mead. Of course, the operators of the Lea were concerned that the New River might drain their river, and the cross flow was carefully regulated using a wonderful and simple device, two chained barges connected to sluice gates which rose and fell with the levels. Then, a hundred years on, six pumping stations were erected along the New River, providing an average daily flow in excess of 22 million gallons.

When the Bridgewater Canal was built near Manchester in 1761, it became clear that the future for the transport of bulk goods over long distances lay by inland waterways. Slowly the countryside was criss-crossed with a network of canals, and a link between the Grand Junction and the Oxford brought prosperity to the south west of Hertfordshire. The first thought was to drive a tunnel close to Langleybury, but in exchange for huge financial compensation (and state-of-the-art landscaping), the Earls of Essex and Clarendon allowed it to run through the parklands of Cassiobury. Slowly the canal was extended through King's Langley, Hemel Hempstead and Berkhamsted. By 1799 it linked at Tring, and after the gargantuan engineering achievement of the Tring Summit level, thus gave access to Birmingham. After a series of financial near-disasters, religious disputes (no traffic movement on Sundays!) and blackmailing landowners, in 1926 it joined with other local canals to form the Grand Union. Through swinging fortunes, it survived; today it is a popular tourist attraction, and is used by recreational narrow boats and cruisers.

BROXBOURNE, *The Lock and the Weir c1955* B413014

In the mid 1800s, the railway from Liverpool Street to Broxbourne provided speedy access to London in the days when a signalman was known as a railway policeman and the engine driver rang a bell to warn his passengers in the open carriages to don their hats before the train moved off!

Transportation of a rather more modern form helped to shape the towns which made up the core of Hertfordshire. The great de Havilland factory at Hatfield provided us with military and civil aircraft. One of the earliest is commemorated by the Comet public house just south of Hatfield on the A1. This is not the passenger-carrying DH106 Comet, but rather its earlier incarnation, the DH88 Comet of 1934, which won the speed prize in the race from Mildenhall to Melbourne in Australia. Hertfordshire also saw the development of the unique wartime Mosquito. This part-wood laminate aircraft was built at Salisbury Hall, just inside the southern boundary of the county. At Leavesden Airfield, Rolls Royce developed a number of aircraft engines from the famous Goblin to the RB211 used on Tristar. The factory closed in 1994 and moved across to another traditional Hertfordshire industry - film making. The giant hangers are ideal for large-scale productions such as the James Bond film 'Goldeneye' and the prequels to 'Star Wars'.

At Stevenage Old Town, the Vincent HRD factory was manufacturing high-quality hand-built motorcycles, including the famous 998cc Black Shadow. A particularly fine example is on display in the Stevenage Museum, which is located in the undercroft of St George's Church.

Hertfordshire does not appear to have had a tradition in automobile manufacturing, although the roads were used for trials of some advanced designs. John Tojeiro, the designer of the world-beating chassis for such cars as the AC Cobra and the Le Mans-challenging Tojeiro Jaguars, used the A1 when he had his workshops at Barkway in the north of Hertfordshire.

There is no question that transportation is and was the lifeblood of Hertfordshire. In the 1930s, 40s and 50s the south east of the county was an almost limitless expanse of glasshouses. The fine quality of the silty soil in the valley of the River Lea was ideal for the market gardening industry, and speedy delivery to the markets in London was imperative if the businesses should reach their full potential. The railways and the rivers gave this communication, and the locality thrived.

The roads, of course, were not always up to the standards set by John Loudon McAdam of Hoddesdon. In 1725, Daniel Defoe wrote of the Great North Road: 'This indeed is a most frightful way if we take it from Hatfield, or rather the park corners of Hatfield House, and from thence to Stevenage ... here is that famous lane called Baldock Lane famous for being impassable that coaches and travellers were obliged to break out of the way even by force ... setting men to take voluntary toll which travellers always chose to pay rather then plunge into sloughs and holes that no horse could wade through.' The condition of the road is hardly surprising. Only a few years later, in 1776, it is recorded that 992,440 beef cattle were driven to Smithfield Market in London, most of them through Hertfordshire. The toll or turnpike systems help to pay for the improvement of the condition of our roads, and by the end of the first quarter of the 19th century the situation was as good as it would be for the next seventy-five years. However, near Liverpool an event was about to take place which would change the whole history of transport not only in Lancashire and Hertfordshire, but all over the world. In 1829, locomotive trials took place at Rainhill.

The first railway through Hertfordshire was the London and Birmingham line, which ran up the west side to Tring. The second Hertfordshire line was planned to run up the eastern boundary from London through Cambridge and on to Yarmouth. It reached Broxbourne in 1840, Harlow in Essex in 1841, and Bishop's Stortford in 1842. Thus by 1843 both the east and west of the county were well served by railways, but there was as yet no railway provision for the centre of the county. A number of proposals had been tabled, but many landowners opposed them, and a state of stalemate appeared to have been reached. A breakthrough came in the late 1840s, when it was agreed that a line could cross the valley of the Mimram to the east of Welwyn. This led to one of Hertfordshire's major engineering triumphs - the Digswell or

Welwyn Viaduct and the tunnels to its north (these were constructed to avoid damage to the estates and parks of the local landed gentry). The line through Hatfield, Welwyn, Knebworth and Stevenage to Peterborough was opened in 1850.

From the south-eastern part of Hertfordshire, our journey takes us across the southern boundary almost parallel to the modern M25. It is here that we meet another of those changes that are so characteristic of the development and change in the county's built environment. The church built in the 1960s at Borehamwood (or is it Boreham Wood? Hertfordshire town and village names are full of uncertainties) is the first of the new ones that we will come across. There is another at Potters Bar and a third at Stevenage. And only St George's at Stevenage was built to serve a new town.

Whilst Borehamwood enjoyed its new church and its fame as a thriving film and TV making centre - the studios, along with Leavesden, are responsible for 'Star Wars' and James Bond films - nearby Elstree was quietly destroying its

ST ALBANS, *Market Place c1950* S2075

historic buildings. This destruction and abandonment of towns, villages and dwellings is a common feature running through the history of Hertfordshire. Maybe the first great planned urban development (and the first to be abandoned) was the Roman city of Verulamium. It was a town to challenge the ideals of Ebenezer Howard and his Garden City movement, and was perhaps the Roman equivalent of the modern new Stevenage. Verulamium has all but disappeared. There are a few mounds outside St Albans, a few bricks and tiles robbed to build the abbey and St Peter's Church, a few keyhole glimpses provided by archaeologists, and a few items displayed in the newly refurbished museum - but little else.

The need for new towns has been a driving force in the evolution of Hertfordshire. To the north of Borehamwood, Elstree and, of course, South Mimms (or is it Mymms? The old problem again) lay the quiet market town of Hatfield. It was, one feels, originally designed to support the Cecil family at the Hatfield House estate. Then, in the 1950s and 1960s the new town of Hatfield sprang up, filled with young and, it should be said, relatively affluent families for whom the Second World War was only a childhood memory. There was good employment in the aircraft and support industries. The skies were always blue - it is rare to find a photograph showing any sign of rain!

A few miles up the A1, we pass another, slightly different town. This is one of Ebenezer Howard's Garden Cities - Welwyn Garden City. Letchworth, in the north of the county but still on the A1, likes to call itself the First Garden City, so one can suppose that Welwyn is the Second Garden City. There is no shame in being second, for the problems and difficulties had been ironed out, and only Letchworthians would dispute that Welwyn is the more spacious and less claustrophobic. The Garden City should not be confused with the nearby village of Welwyn a couple of miles to the west. Welwyn village has benefited from the rise of the Garden City. It is an unspoiled community with many original houses and shops. Although the church has undergone huge changes, it still retains the air of late medieval tranquillity. Along with Codicote, a few miles to the north west, Welwyn demonstrates an unchanging aspect of Hertfordshire.

The new towns along the A1, the old Great North Road, are like a string of pearls, for they occur with regularity and with only a small gap between. Indeed, trapped between the first and second garden cities lies Stevenage, which until the 1950s was a busy but smallish market town straddling a rather congested road. For some of us its claim to fame was the Vincent HRD motorcycle works, but most people visited it for its unique market and shops. However, like an explosion, the new town burst on the hamlets, greens, 'ends' and open fields to the south east, and seemingly overnight the Hertfordshire accent was replaced by the unfamiliar voices of Londoners. Industry arrived, and factories and offices filled the strip of land between the Old North Road, the railway and the new town. There was employment for all and clean country air, polluted only by the increased traffic and the occasional factory chimney.

Our journey has taken us on a U-shaped route down the east side of Hertfordshire, across the southern border to the west side, and finally northwards up the central core. What have we seen? Not too many green fields, but rather a landscape which has seen, and continues to see, major change. Much of the original landscape has been lost - we have seen little from pre-Roman times. Indeed, the first influx of urban and rural development must be laid at the door of the Romano-British people. In many areas the evidence lies only a few feet below the surface. From the great city of Verulamium, via the bath-house at Welwyn down to the occasional finds of coins along Ermine Street, the Romans seem to be struggling to tell us about themselves.

Successive wars and monarchs have left their mark - King Alfred and the Danes on the River Lea; Earl Harold's English army racing south-wards through Hertfordshire in a state of euphoria after its success at Stamford Bridge, but on its way to ultimate defeat at Hastings in 1066; the deaths of pretenders to the throne at St Albans and Barnet; and Elizabeth I receiving the news of her accession at Hatfield. Indeed, the birth of another Queen Elizabeth took place in Hertfordshire at St Paul's Walden.

What will future historians say about Hertfordshire? What evidence for the original county will survive? Stevenage's expansion, which began in the last century, continues; new roads are planned; industrial estates take over greenfield sites; the government imposes 50,000 new dwellings in Hertfordshire. Soon the central part of Hertfordshire, in particular, could become a concrete plain. But the underlying heritage and history will never be destroyed.

Hertfordshire is a county of contrasts. It can be attractive, or it can be depressingly grim; but in the words of Candide, it enjoys 'the best of all possible worlds'.

ST ALBANS, *Holywell Hill 1921* 70480

DOWN THE EASTERN SIDE

ROYSTON, *Kneesworth Street c1929* 81891

This view will be instantly recognised today. The shop in the centre, which was originally part of the medieval temporary market, is now an accountant's office; a small triangular area has been planted as a memorial to Diana, Princess of Wales. On the left, with its tall chimney, stands King James II's summer palace (next door to the recently erected - in 1929 - gas showrooms). King James was an inveterate hunter, and nearby Therfield Heath provided him with the thrill of the chase. Behind the palace were the royal dog kennels, remembered today in the byway called Dog Kennel Lane; today the Richard Cox House retirement home stands close by.

▶ **ROYSTON,** *The Parish Church 1929* 81902

Originally part of 13th-century Royston Priory, the church was bought by the townsfolk as a parish church for the newly formed town of Royston in the late 1800s. Among those lying in the churchyard is Henry Andrews, the originator of Old Moore's Almanack. A few hundred yards south west of the church is Sun Hill (after which Sun Hill Police Station of television's 'The Bill' was named). One of the houses there was owned by Lord Monteagle, who received the letter revealing the details of the Gunpowder Plot.

▼ **ASHWELL,** *High Street c1951* A149003

In the centre stands the Rose & Crown. In the late 1700s, William Mann was the landlord; he also held the post of Overseer of the Poor, responsible for ensuring the distribution of payments to the paupers. His accounts of 1774 failed to be accepted by the churchwardens, who reported that 'a prosecution should be commenced against William Mann.' On being interviewed, he said that 'he was innocent, that it was thro' the ignorance of his wife and son.' The vestry allowed him to repay £18 13s 1d rather than going to prison.

▶ BARKWAY, *High Street*
c1965 B281016

Barkway High Street is steeped in travel and transport. The village straddled the main route between London, Cambridge and King's Lynn, with up to 32 coaches passing through each day in the early 1800s. On the right is a thatched hall house; behind it is Berg Cottage, where Samuel Pepys is said to have lodged on his way to his family estate at Huntingdon. The thatched cottage in the left middle distance was the home of John Tojeiro, whose workshop behind saw the birth of such famous sports and racing cars as the Ecurie Ecosse Le Mans Jaguars and the successful AC Cobra.

◀ BUNTINGFORD
Market Hill 1923
74923

The Royston Crown newspaper of 19 April 1935 reported: 'A long line of beasts and pens of calves, sheep, pigs and lambs stretching almost the whole length of the Market hill, marked the re-opening of the Buntingford Market on Monday. There was a splendid attendance of buyers, and many neighbouring farmers, dealers and merchants were there to support the re-opening. It was like old times again.'

▲ **BUNTINGFORD,** *Market Hill c1955* B245041

On this sunny spring day, two young motorcyclists stop to pass the time of day outside the shop between the Bull and the Master Tanner's House. Behind this house stood a tannery with buildings running down to the banks of the River Rib. The bark was taken from the local oak trees and soaked in lime baths. The raw hides were then steeped in the liquid to make tanned leather.

BUNTINGFORD, *The Town Clock c1955*
▶ B245010

It seems that the people of Buntingford needed only to know the approximate time, for the Town Clock has only an hour hand! It is mounted over the passageway between the early Crowned Lyon Inn (later Day's newspaper and sweet shop) and the Angel Inn (now a hairdressing salon). The townspeople are justly proud of their clock, and it has recently undergone a major restoration paid for by public subscription. However, to indicate a more accurate time, a new Millennium Clock (this time two-handed) has been installed on the pavement outside the Bull.

BENINGTON
Benington Lordship
c1960 B406001

Benington Lordship has the air of an ancient monument surrounded by Saxon mounds and fishponds. However, very little of the Norman keep survives, and this gateway, although it looks authentic, is actually a 19th-century sham. Even the much admired and visited gardens are a relatively modern addition, having been laid out a hundred years ago by Arthur Bott on what had been a bowling green.

STANDON, *The Church c1965* S377001

Unique in Hertfordshire, Standon parish church has a detached bell tower and a porch at the west end rather than on the south wall. It is built on the side of a hill, and a flight of steps lead up from the nave to the altar. Although the building dates from the 14th century, the foundations are Saxon. It is said to have been built by the Knights Hospitallers as a 'processional' church, one of only three in England.

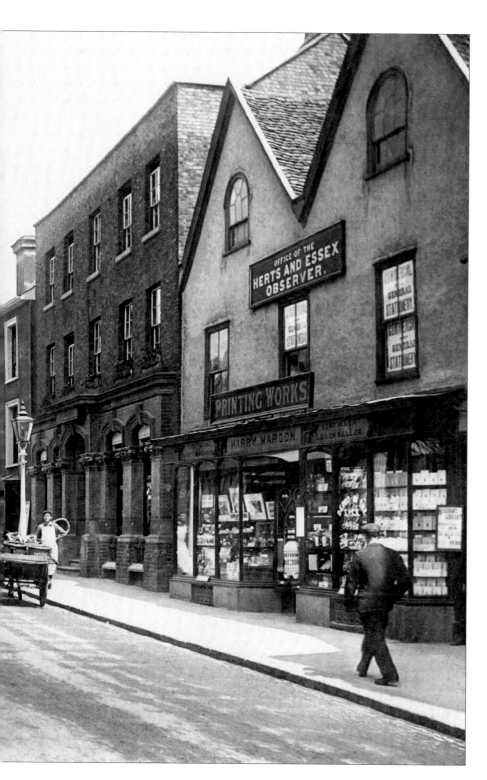

BISHOP'S STORTFORD
North Street 1903 49755

The statue of a white hart, which can be seen over the door of the premises of Mr Holland in the middle distance, originally stood at the barracks of the 1st Herts Light Horse Volunteers. It was later moved two buildings along the street, and now surmounts the entrance to Boardman's bookshop. The water pump (left) was later removed, and now stands in the new cemetery.

23

▶ **BISHOP'S STORTFORD,** *The River c1950* B104004

By the1950s, the malting industry, which had been the main source of the town's wealth, had all but disappeared. The River Stort was silting up, and a steam dredger was needed to keep the passage clear. Many barges were moored at the derelict quayside, and the cranes used for hoisting the sacks of malt had become rusted and silent. Today the river is slowly coming to life again with pleasure craft and a little commercial traffic.

▼ **SAWBRIDGEWORTH,** *The Church of Great St Mary 1903* 51101

One of the finest parish churches in Hertfordshire, St Mary's boasts a renowned collection of brasses and sculptures. Deceptively modest from the outside, the interior is huge and impressive. The church stands on an expanse of lawn surrounded by pine and yew trees. The churchyard gives fine views across the River Stort. Sawbridgeworth is said to be the location for the first fruit farm nursery in England. Founded in 1725 by John Rivers, the nursery developed many strains of fruit trees, and a number still carry the name.

▶ **WARE,** *A Gazebo on the River Lea 1925* 77116

The gazebos are a unique feature on the banks of the Lea at Ware. Although they exist on other rivers in Britain, nowhere else has such a fine collection. Ware's gazebos were built at the ends of the long gardens attached to the houses and shops in the High Street. In the 1830s, the writer James Smith records that there were twenty-five of these 'little Dutch summerhouses'. This pretty white-boarded gazebo, reflected in the Lea, was owned by the Harradence family in the 1890s.

◀ **WARE**
High Street 1929
81840

Looking eastwards along the High Street, we can see a couple of loafers leaning against the corner of the local pub. Here, a few years previously, there had been a sign advertising 'Livery & Bait Stables. Horses & Carriages for Hire'; but with the arrival of the motor car, the stables were redundant, and at this date the establishment boasts only 'Dunvilles VR Whisky' and 'McMullens Stout'. The white building on the corner of East Street had been a tea rooms - 'Caterers for Parties, etc' - but, in 1925 was an ironmonger's and hardware shop. Around 1927, it reverted to a baker's shop, and once again offered genteel afternoon tea for visitors.

▼ **HERTFORD,** *The War Memorial 1933* 85535

The memorial to those who fell during the two World Wars stands in the middle of Parliament Square. It was sculpted by Alfred Drury to a design by Sir Aston Webb; it was unveiled in November 1921, initially recording the names of those killed in the Great War. Over the years, the raised area around the base has been shaved away - today, the memorial stands in the centre of a busy traffic island. Despite many attempts to move it (and a number of assaults by heavy lorries), the memorial has survived.

► **HERTFORD,** *Fore Street 1933* 85534

At the junction of Fore Street and Market Street, Dyers' and Sinden's shops (previously Neale's furniture stores) display a fine example of traditional Hertfordshire and Essex pargeting. After the upper floors of the building had been rendered, the soft plaster was moulded and shaped into intricate patterns and swags. Occasionally these bold statements of success and affluence are painted; in this case, they have been left in their natural colour.

► **HODDESDON**
Dobbs Weir c1955
H259038

The River Lea and the New River form the boundary between Hertfordshire and Essex. Both counties can justifiably claim the New River as their own. Dobbs Weir, sometimes known as the Tumbling Bay, lies near Rye House and the delightfully named Carthagena Lock. There had been a ford here with a small wooden bridge, but this fell into decay and a new, more permanent structure was built. Because the water near the weir was so shallow, when the river froze for 68 days in 1891 the ice was so thick that the local people were able to skate from one side to the other. Later, in the 1900s, Dobbs Weir was the site of illuminated river carnivals.

◄ **HODDESDON,** *The Roman Road c1950* H259006

Ermine Street, the Roman road, runs as straight as an arrow northwards through Broxbourne woods to the west of Hoddesdon. It can still be traced a few hundred yards to the west of Goose Green where it crosses Lord Street/Mangrove Lane. One short stretch, at the westernmost point of Cock Lane near White Stubbs Lane, continues today as metalled road. In the north of Hertfordshire, Ermine Street slices through the old Hundred of Edwinstree. It is said that Edwinstree took its name from a very slurred pronunciation of 'Ermine Street.'

▲ **HODDESDON,** *The Tower Centre 1968* H259120

Tower Heights (later known as the Tower Centre), a complex of 54 flats, 32 shops and parking for 242 cars, was completed in 1967 at a cost of £1.5 million. The architects were E S Boyer & Partners for Heron Developments, who ran the service station on the ground floor adjacent to Burford Street. Although feted as a great success, Heron Developments sold the property shortly afterwards; despite numerous attempts by the local council, the centre has never attained its full potential.

◄ **HODDESDON,** *The Pavilion Cinema and the Clock Tower c1950* H259009

The Pavilion Cinema was opened in 1938 in part of the old Christies Brewery to replace the original cinema founded in 1913. The old cinema became the Robert Gilling Hall, the headquarters of the Haileybury Boys' Club. In turn, the Pavilion closed in 1972 and was converted into a bingo hall. It appears that this photograph was taken on a quiet Sunday afternoon, as there is no sign of busy traffic or the bustling market. The young men on the left may be waiting for Jack's Tea and Coffee Bar to open. Jack's and the buildings round the base of the clock tower were demolished in 1965 to make way for the new building development to which the clock tower gave its name.

▼ **HODDESDON,** *The War Memorial and the White Swan Inn c1965* H259123

Like most communities, Hoddesdon suffered the loss of many young men and women in the First World War. The memorial was erected in 1921, and further names were added after the Second World War. The war effort touched Hoddesdon in another way, for a factory produced large numbers of Nissen huts at nearby Rye Park. The White Swan was built in the early 1500s, and served as a meeting place for the traders and cattlemen attending the town market. The inn was refurbished in 1963, when the barns at the rear were demolished to make space for a car park.

▶ **HODDESDON,** *High Street looking North 1959* H259073

At the north end of the town, the High Street split, with the western fork leading to Ware and on to Cambridge and the eastern branch to Stanstead St Margarets and the Hadhams. The Ware road dipped northwards past the terraced cottages in Amwell Street on the west and the more upmarket town houses on the High Pavement (now part of the Tower Centre). It ran down to the crossing of the Woollens Brook close to the site of the modern Dinant Link Road roundabout. The traffic is remarkably quiet - nothing appears to be moving on the road. A late model Vauxhall PA Cresta (probably black and green) blocks the bus stop, and a Ford 105E Anglia stands under the no waiting sign. Above the Sainsbury's lorry, the tower of Hoddesdon parish church stands proudly on the skyline.

HODDESDON, *Market Place looking North c1955* H259036

In the far distance stands the Maidenhead Inn with the Clock Tower in front. The Maidenhead, dating from before 1576, was destroyed in 1964 to make way for the Tower Centre. The Clock Tower is a replacement for the original, demolished in 1835. It had been the Chapel of St Katherine at a time when Hoddesdon was part of the parish of Great Amwell. The last religious service was recorded in 1706. The new tower, later to become known as the Town Hall, was built by public subscription the following year - local landowners and businessmen donated bricks. On the left is the Bull Hotel, demolished in 1964 - its sign is now in the Lowewood Museum collection. On the right, to the north of the very fine early 1950s Humber Super Snipe/Pullman, the market stalls are sited exactly where traders have bargained and sold for at least 500 years. The Humber is rivalled only by the 1951 Jaguar Mark 5 convertible parked outside the baker's.

HODDESDON, *High Street looking North c1950* H259011

The Golden Lion on the left of this view was known as the White Hind before 1535 and continued under this name until at least 1667. Many buildings then had names, and there is no evidence to suggest that the White Hind was an inn at that time. Possibly the earliest mention of the name Golden Lion was in 1756. The gap next to the Golden Lion is due to bomb damage sustained in May 1941. The pedestrians and motorists pay little attention to the rules of the road. Were the two ladies crossing from the right mown down by the black Wolseley or by the Panther motorcycle? Did they manage to nip across the High Street and disappear between the two Morris 8s parked across the pedestrian crossing? It is no wonder that the whole of this area was changed in the 1960s; this stretch of the High Street eventually became one-way.

► **HODDESDON**
High Street looking South 1964 H259122

Photographed at an important moment of change, the High Street appears tranquil and unaware of the turmoil to come! Only the white facade of the Bull Inn (right) remains; the sign has been removed and will eventually find its way to Lowewood Museum. Behind the photographer, the surveyors and architects are greedily eyeing the Maidenhead and preparing for its demolition and the erection of the Tower Centre, and making ready for the huge increase in traffic. Between 1827 and 1836, the building just past the gabled Post Office (centre left) was the home of John Loudon McAdam, the 'Colossus of Roads', who pioneered the modern method of road building. His basic method is still used today; indeed, the High Street had been built to his standard.

◄ **HODDESDON**
The Spinning Wheel Gardens c1965 H259129

What is today known as the Spinning Wheel was built in 1870 by Septimus Warner, brother of the bellfounder John Warner, whose works were in London and Felixstowe. Now a Citizen's Advice Bureau and residential flats, it backs onto the popular local swimming pool. The gardens of Italian Cottage, as it was originally known, extended for about two acres, but these have been pared back, and today little more than is shown in the photograph survives.

▲ **BROXBOURNE,** *St Augustine's Parish Church c1955* B413007

Situated close to the site of Broxbourne Mill and directly opposite the New River, much of the structure of St Augustine's dates from the early 15th century. A major restoration was carried out in 1855, and the unique Say Chapel, added in 1522, was restored in 1993. In the time of the staunchly Roman Catholic Queen Mary (1553-1558), it was said that the incumbent had been dismissed because he and others had 'married or otherwise slanderingly deceived themselves'. When the vicarage (right) was renovated in 1962, the rendering was removed to reveal a timber-framed house of an earlier period than had previously been thought.

◄ **BROXBOURNE**
St John's Parade, High Road c1955 B413022

The parade was built in the early 1930s to provide shops for the new houses being built in the expanding community at Broxbourne. It was named after the local auctioneer and land agent, F R St John. As well as the usual grocer, fruiterer, post office and newsagent, the parade contained Matthias Cycle Repairs and Sales (second from the left); this was a very necessary service when so few people owned cars.

33

BROXBOURNE, *The New River c1955* B413012

Neither new nor a river, the New River was constructed in 1613 to
provide a source of clean water for London. The concept of a fresh
water supply for the capital was first seriously discussed by Edmund
Colthurst, but it was Sir Hugh Myddleton who was the driving force
behind the project. Of course, the local people objected to Londoners
having their water. Nonetheless, the project was completed. The
New River takes a convoluted 20-mile route from the Lee Navigation
(between Hertford and Ware) to London. It follows the contours,
sometimes via underground culverts, so that there is no sudden drop,
and now ends at Stoke Newington Coppermills treatment centre.

BROXBOURNE, *The Lock and the Weir c1955* B413014

The River Lea runs almost parallel to the New River through Broxbourne and Cheshunt. The Lea was a popular leisure attraction for local people and Londoners. In the early part of the last century, at Easter and Bank Holidays swarms of visitors came by train from the capital to walk the tow path, hire pleasure boats or to dance at Rye Park.

► BROXBOURNE
The River Lea c1960
B413031

Close to this haven for narrow boats and pleasure craft is the place where King Alfred is said to have split the river when he was defending the country from the Danes. As the river flows south, it divided into a number of smaller channels such as the Horse Mill Stream, the Corn Mill Stream and the Small River Lea. Although the river is known as the Lea, the organisation which oversees water management in the area is known as the Lee Conservancy Board. No one seems to know why there is the difference in spelling - but get it wrong in correspondence at your peril!

◄ **BROXBOURNE**
The Cheshunt Bulb Co, High Road c1940
B413024

Smallbrook Farm, the white building in the centre of the photograph, stands next to the entrance to the Cheshunt Bulb Co's shop. The gardens at the junction of the High Road and New Road were renowned for their high quality Dutch bulbs. In the distance is the George pub; peeping over the trees are the chimneys of the houses of the expensive St Catharine's Estate.

NEW ROAD

BROXBOURNE, *Van Hage's Nursery, High Road c1965* B413125

About twenty-five years after B413024 (preceding page) was taken, the
general shape of the plot has hardly changed, but Van Hage's have taken
over the business from the Cheshunt Bulb Co. The High Road is a little
busier - note the RT London Transport bus. Van Hage's was an exciting
venue for families at the weekend, and, as the author remembers, very
busy on the day before Mothers' Day! Van Hage's now operate from Amwell
Hill, south of Ware, where the windmill continues to attract the discerning
gardener and, at weekends, the narrow gauge railway entrances the
children.

BROXBOURNE, *High Road c1955* B413044

This row of shops and offices stands on the High Road close
to the junction with Station Road leading across the railway to
Nazing in Essex. Although much of Broxbourne has changed over
the past fifty years, this view is instantly recognisable today. Only
the trees surrounding Deaconsfield (in the distance, right), which
have now been cut back, and a remarkable lack of traffic, give a
clue to the 1950s date.

▼ WORMLEY, *St Lawrence's Church 1955* W297015

The 12th-century church of St Lawrence originally had a flint and stone tower, but this was demolished in 1826 to make way for the small stone gable we see here. The church was enlarged in 1862 and the west wall of the nave rebuilt. At the same time, a particularly fine wrought iron screen was installed in the chancel. In 1963, the stone gable was removed and a wooden bellcote was added, topped with a gold-painted replica of the 1706 weathervane.

► WORMLEY, *Church Lane c1955* W297002

Church Lane leads westwards from the village past Wormleybury, with its 11th-century Church of St Lawrence, through Carneles Green to Baas Hill. It was a favourite Sunday walk for families and courting couples. Here we can see one of the lodges to Wormleybury (left) and the road crossing the bridge over the river which fed the great lake in the park. In colder weather, the frozen lake was taken over by skaters and very occasionally opened to the villagers. Today the Church Lane walk is still popular; although the lane crosses over the A10 motorway, it is a peaceful place for picnics and impromptu outings.

◄ WORMLEY
High Road c1955
W297013

Shaw the newsagent's, part of this block erected in the mid 1930s, continued to occupy the corner of the High Road and Wharf Road until the late 1960s. Previously it had been the site of Mr Smith the wheelwright's workshop and smithy. Opposite the Ford E83W van is the Old Star pub. In the 1920s, the New Star and the Old Star pubs stood cheek-by-jowl, but in 1937, the New Star closed, and the Old Star was the survivor. Wharf Road leads down to the River Lea close to Kings Wear and the Nazeing Marshes.

► CHESHUNT, *St Mary's Church*
c1955 C319006

Building work began at St Mary's in 1418 on the site of an earlier church; it was completed in 1438. The church tower contains an interesting peal of eight bells, all of which were recast by Gillett & Johnson of Croydon in 1911. The memorials in the body of the church are particularly fine, and include a monument to Henry Atkins, court physician in the time of the Stuarts. An early forerunner of Cheshunt's market garden industry, the appropriately named Nehemiah Grew also has a memorial. Grew was one of the first researchers into the taxonomy of flowers, plants and trees, and often lectured to the Royal Society.

▼ **CHESHUNT,** *Bishop's College c1955* C319007

Bishop's College was, until its move to Cambridge in 1905, the non-conformist Cheshunt College. It then formed the Church of England Bishop's Theological College from 1909 to 1968. Cheshunt Council bought the college in 1972 and it was extended to become the main offices of Broxbourne Borough Council when Broxbourne, Cheshunt and Hoddesdon combined to form the new borough of Broxbourne. The present buildings were opened by the Duke of Kent in 1986.

► **CHESHUNT**
The New River
c1960 C319033

Nowhere in Cheshunt is far from the New River. Here we see the tranquil and almost still river as it passes to the east of the Bishop's College. Part of the little wooden bridge survives today, but the attractive brick and flint building to its left was demolished around 1983 after the Borough of Broxbourne took over the towpath and surrounding gardens.

◄ **CHESHUNT,** *Temple Bar, Theobalds c1955*
C319038

When the reigning monarch wishes to enter the City of London, he or she must wait at the top of Fleet Street to receive the Sword of the City and to be given permission to pass. Originally the monarch passed through Temple Bar, designed in 1672 by Sir Christopher Wren, but it was removed in 1872 when it become a hazard to traffic. The numbered stones were put into store, and in 1886 Sir Henry Meux bought them and had them erected as a gate to his estate at Theobalds for his wife, Lady Valerie. In the summer of 2003, Temple Bar in Theobalds Park was taken down stone by stone and re-erected in Paternoster Square in London, near St Paul's Cathedral. The project was completed in November 2004.

► **CHESHUNT,** *The Public Library c1955* C319015

The library, part funded by a gift to the people of Cheshunt by the Andrew Carnegie Foundation, was opened to the public in 1907. Designed by J Myrtle Smith, the library included a School of Art. Every detail in the building was crafted with a meticulous eye for design; the banisters on the stairs, the handles to the doors, the stained glass windows, all were manufactured for this specific building to the highest possible standard. The first librarian was Oswald C Hudson. He was given a magnificent annual grant of £14 to purchase new books. Such was the demand from the expanding population that new wings were added (after this photograph was taken) in 1956.

CHESHUNT, *The Grammar School c1955* C319017

Cheshunt Modern School in Windmill Lane was completed in 1938 - its first headmaster was R J Moxom. Very soon afterwards it was extended and renamed Cheshunt County School. Later it became Cheshunt Grammar School, and later, after considerable protest from local people and in particular ex-pupils, the name changed to Cheshunt Comprehensive School. The school closed in 1992, and the whole establishment moved to its new home in College Road. In 1997, the old Cheshunt School building was demolished and replaced with housing.

CHESHUNT, *High Street c1965* C319047

We are looking north along the High Street, where the buildings are little different today. Some of the shop names have changed, but many of the businesses in 1965 would have been familiar to Cheshunt people 100 years ago. T Taylor's butcher's shop is recorded in the 1890s. On the other hand, Bancrofts were H Bullard in 1930, and the shop between was a newsagent's which allowed you to 'Telephone from Here'. Frith's photograph is a delight for motoring historians. From the left is a 105E Anglia Estate, a Morris Minor Traveller, a Ford Consul, a Morris Commercial and a Bedford CAV. In the distance is another Ford 100E with a Vauxhall PA approaching us. That must be one of the last of Cheshunt Dairies' horse-drawn milk floats resting in the lay-by next to Cadmore Lane (right).

CHESHUNT, *Wolsey Hall c1965*
C319043

Built in 1961 to provide a public venue in Cheshunt, Wolsey Hall in Windmill Lane has seen the early years of some of Britain's most successful pop groups. Cliff Richard and the Shadows were amongst the first performers. Hank Marvin, lead guitarist of the Shadows, visited later with his own group. In October 1964, The Who performed on stage at Wolsey Hall. In the early 1990s, your author gave a lecture at Wolsey Hall - the audience was around 30. The Who attracted an audience well into three figures! The lady with the Silver Cross pram is about to pass the very contemporary 298cc Isetta bubble car (on the extreme left hand side of this view) in the car-park.

CHESHUNT, *Grundy Park c1955* C319002

Originally one of the largest country houses in Cheshunt, Grundy Park is now home to one of the Borough of Broxbourne's leisure centres. The grounds face westwards towards Turner's Hill; they are still attractive public gardens, but the fine topiary has disappeared. The greenhouses (right) provided particularly fine blossoms throughout the year, and were popular during civic gatherings. Just to the south of Grundy Park stood Elm Arches, which was given to Cheshunt in 1911. It was mysteriously burnt down in the late 1980s and a plaque was erected to its memory. The original terracotta plaque, now in Lowewood Museum at Hoddesdon, was manufactured by the famous firm of Pulhams, whose works stood close to Broxbourne railway station; the replacement (of fibreglass resin) was made by Alex Duckworth of Barkway. In the grounds to the north east of Grundy Park lies Wolsey Hall, and to the south is Cheshunt Public Library.

CHESHUNT, *Turner's Hill c1965* C319051

Newnham Parade was built in the early 1960s on the site of the old Triangle Café, which had been demolished in 1960. The Triangle was a favourite meeting place for locals and travellers from London to Ware. The fountain stands on the roundabout. In the 1990s this was the subject of occasional comment by residents, who complained that the water height was not quite up to standard. An officer of the local council was deputised to be the 'fountain monitor' who recorded the force each day. In winter, when the fountain froze, this was a particularly challenging responsibility.

WALTHAM CROSS, *The Four Swans Hotel c1950* W163007

The Austin saloon passes southwards under the sign of the four swans towards the Eleanor Cross. The strange network of overhead cabling is the wiring for the trolley bus service from London which terminated here. The original wooden swans on the sign are now displayed at the Lowewood Museum at Hoddesdon; today a new beam is surmounted by a set of fibreglass swans. The wooden swans made a fine target for lads with catapults. Today, the fibreglass replacements carry out the same function - one of the heads is missing!

WALTHAM CROSS

The Queen Eleanor Cross c1921 70171

Twelve crosses were erected in the 1290s to commemorate the resting place of the body of Queen Eleanor, wife of Edward I, as it was brought to London for burial in December 1290. Over the past couple of hundred years, this cross has been regularly cleaned and restored, although for a period in the 1700s it was badly neglected and damaged by iconoclasts. The figures in the niches have been replaced by facsimiles. In the background, behind the Manchester-built Model T Ford, is the Waltham Cross branch of the London Joint Stock Bank - it was later to become part of the Midland Bank. The Tailor and Hosier shop (left) was Haynes's toyshop and tobacconist's in 1960.

▶ **POTTERS BAR**
The Cenotaph 1967
P131045

When Frith's photographer took his picture of the war memorial at the junction of the Causeway leading to Northaw and the Hatfield Road (or Great North Road), he called it the cenotaph - 'the empty tomb'. The memorial stands on the site of the original toll house which later became a sweet shop and tea rooms known as the Cyclist's Rest. It was demolished in 1896. It is said that the famous 18th-century highwayman Dick Turpin, on Black Bess, jumped over the toll bar on his frantic ride from London to York.

◄ **POTTERS BAR,** *The Railway Station c1965*
P131040

The London to York railway was built in 1850 to supplement the road taken by Dick Turpin and Black Bess. As Potters Bar developed, it was decided in 1938 that an improved station should be built, but the declaration of war in 1939 delayed it. This station, used in the photograph by one of the new diesel locomotives, was completed in 1959. It was the site of a number of tragic accidents: in 1899 the Earl of Stafford was killed, in 1946 two members of staff died, and in May 2002 seven passengers and staff lost their lives when the express train from London to Kings Lynn was derailed as it passed through the station.

POTTERS BAR, *Darkes Lane, looking North 1967* P131030

In the 1960s, Potters Bar was a prosperous commuter town on the main railway line giving speedy access to London. But even thirty-five years ago, the motor car held sway over the main roads. However, unlike today, most of the vehicles are parked, and only two appear to be on the move. This photograph is a motor historian's delight, with at least three Ford 300E vans parked on the right, a black Austin A55, a (possibly puce and white) Vauxhall VX 4/90, an Austin A40, two Ford 105E Anglias (one an estate car), and a Vauxhall PA Cresta. These cars were serviced by the Shell garage in the far right distance next door to Goulds, the shoe shop, Cullingford and Smiths, and Drays, the confectioner's.

POTTERS BAR, *Darkes Lane, looking South 1967* P131042

The busy shopping centre contained many familiar shops. Some of them are now just memories, such as F W Woolworth, Mac Fisheries (a Findus delivery van is making a delivery), Payantake Stores and Peter Goodfellow. A branch of Lloyds Bank stands among the buildings on the left, and the Electricity Board showrooms are in the far distance on the right. The Ritz cinema, built in 1934, is the site of Tesco. In the far distance stands the railway bridge by the station - the site of the tragic accident in 2002 where some of the debris from the derailed train fell and killed a passer-by.

▼ **POTTERS BAR,** *The Church of the Vincentian Spanish Fathers c1965*
P131049

In 1922 the Vincentian Spanish Fathers acquired a plot of land at Hillside in Barnet Road
to provide a training facility for young priests to foreign missions. The new building was
completed in 1925, but was destroyed by a V2 rocket in 1945. Several people were killed and
much damage was done to local property. In 1960 a new church, designed by Felix Velerde,
was built at a cost of £40,000 and dedicated to St Vincent de Paul and St Louis de Marillac.

▶ **POTTERS BAR,** *Wyllyotts
Manor c1955* P131012

This partly 16th-century timber-
framed building is named after
the Wylyot or Williot family, who
held the manor in the mid 1300s
as an outlier of the manor of
South Mimms. The property was
once owned by Alderman James
Hickson, a city brewer, who left
it to the Brewers Company to
support six almshouses in South
Mimms. In 1965 the complex
was wholly occupied as council
offices, but today it contains a
restaurant and cinema. Also on
the site stands the fine museum
of the Potters Bar and District
Historical Society, which opened
in 1990.

◀ **POTTERS BAR,** *The Farm at St Raphael's Centre, Barvin Park c1950* P131001

In 1930, the Hospitaller Order of St John of God agreed to build St Raphael's Residential Training Centre at Barvin Park on Coopers Lane Road. Opened by Cardinal Bourne in October 1931, the centre was to provide 'a colony in England for Catholic male adult mental defectives and epileptics'. The residents were taught horticulture and farming. A new chapel was dedicated in August 1936 with an adjacent cemetery. In 1984 the first females were admitted. Within 10 years, the centre was closed; 'after an extensive resettlement and training programme, residents were accommodated and supported in their own homes within the community.' But for many of the residents, the centre had been their home.

► **POTTERS BAR,** *Oakmere House c1965*
P131047

Built around 1800, the original Oakmere House was destroyed by fire whilst being extended. The new building was occupied in the 1900s by the Forbes family; Eileen Baillie recalls old Mrs E M Forbes 'lying on an elegant couch ... having her beautiful hair dressed by her maid in a silvery crown over her head.' The winters were particularly cold, and when the lake froze over Mrs Forbes let the local people skate there. In 1916, the L31 Zeppelin was shot down and crashed nearby. The locals rushed to wake Mrs Forbes, who appeared at the door in her nightclothes. The excited people told her what had happened, but annoyed at being woken, she told them: 'All right, we will see to it in the morning!' and slammed the door in their faces. Parts of the Zeppelin can be seen in Potters Bar's fine museum at the Wyllyotts Centre. In the 1980s, Oakmere House was converted to a Beefeater restaurant.

THE SOUTH AND WEST

BUSHEY
The Masonic Senior Boys School c1955
B414017

The school was founded in 1798 at Wood Green in
north London. The construction of the new buildings
on the site of a Jacobean house on the Grange Estate at
Bushey began in 1898, and the school took possession
in 1902/03. Over 400 boys were accommodated in each
of the Senior and Junior Schools. The Masonic School
closed in 1977.

BUSHEY, *The Parish Church of St James c1955* B414020

Before the restoration work of 1870, the interior of the church
contained tightly packed box pews and a rood loft. These were
removed; of the original fittings, only the ancient pulpit and the
fine brass chandelier, dating from 1727, survive. The chandelier,
reminiscent of the one in Van Eyck's painting of the Arnolfini wedding,
was a gift from Richard Capper. It had been discarded during the
renovations, but was rescued; by 1898, it was in very poor condition
and covered in verdigris. Fortunately it has now been restored to its
former glory, and hangs proudly from the ceiling of the nave.

WATFORD, *Whippendell Woods 1921* 70496

Daniel Defoe, in his 'Tour through the Islands of Great Britain' of 1724-
26, describes Whippendell Woods as 'one of the finest near London'.
The woods were bought by Watford Urban District Council as 'parkland
for public use' in 1935. They had been part of the Cassiobury estate,
once owned by the Earls of Essex, but had been retained by the owners
when the council took the main part of the estate between 1913 and
1930. Whippendell had narrowly missed destruction in the late 1800s
when it was proposed that a new railway should cut through the
woods, but the owner fought the proposal and they were saved.

▲ **WATFORD**
The Pond 1906 53625

The railings around the pond were extended in 1914 to prevent accidents during the blackout. It was thought likely that Zeppelins would use the lighted town as either a target or a navigational aid; all homes and public buildings had their light extinguished during night-time, or had their windows blocked with heavy dark curtains. During the late 1920s a parade of shops and a cinema were built over the wooded area on the left, and the pond was landscaped and a fountain installed. Fifty years later, the area was 'upgraded' and is now open-plan.

▶ RADLETT
Christ Church c1960
R267029

Christ Church is believed to stand on the site of an ancient chantry chapel. It was built in 1864 and extended in 1907. The bells have an interesting history. The single bell of 1864, cast by John Warner who lived at Hoddesdon, was replaced by a set of eight tubular steel bells in 1899. In 1938, these were removed and a gramophone, with amplifier, was installed to play the sound of bells ringing. Finally, in 1964, a peal of six real bells were installed.

◄ CHORLEYWOOD, *The Common 1903* 49310

It is thought that the common was originally used as a foraging ground for pigs: the Rickmansworth entry of the Domesday Book reads 'Woodland for a thousand and two hundred pigs'. In more recent times, the trees and scrub were cleared, and the common was used for grazing sheep and cattle on their way to market. Up to 1914, the lords of the manor were the Gilliat family, but it eventually came into the hands of Chorley Urban District Council. Although the 'commoners' retained their grazing rights, the common has now been landscaped; part is used as a public golf course, whilst the north-east corner is occupied by the excellent Christ Church C of E Primary School founded in 1853.

▼ **RADLETT,** *Canons Close c1960* R267028

Canons Close is a quiet cul-de-sac tucked behind Shenley Hill and Craigwell Avenue.
This leafy junction typifies the quiet affluence of the residential area away from the main
shopping centres strung along Watling Street. An early Austin A40 Farina, with its sprightly 'A'
Series engine, makes light work of the incline as it prepares to turn off into the close.

▶ **RADLETT,** *Watling Street c1954*
R267007

The main thoroughfare follows the route
of the Roman Watling Street. Nothing
in this view would suggest a historical
background to the community, although
the old saloon car in the centre reminds
us of wartime motoring. Ten years after
peace was declared, it still sports the
white-edged mudguards which were so
familiar during the blackout. The two
young lads have possibly taken a cycle
ride out to Radlett from north London.
The sporty drop-handlebar touring
cycle is parked by the roadside using the
traditional 'pedal on the kerb' method,
whilst the more sedate roadster rests
against the park bench. The cyclists take
a breather to read the Hotspur or the
Wizard.

◄ **SANDRIDGE**
St Leonard's Church
c1962 S375301

St Leonard's is one of the oldest parish churches in Hertfordshire. It was founded early in the 12th century as a chapel to St Albans. The chancel was built in 1400 by Abbot John Moote. The original spire collapsed in 1688/93 and was replaced with a cupola in 1786, restored in 1837. In 1886 it, in turn, was demolished, and the broach spire was added in 1887. The churchyard was cleared around 1960, and the beds of daffodils were created in memory of a local inhabitant. In the distance stands the lych gate, with the Queens Head behind, and the enclosure containing the war memorial and garden of remembrance.

► **ST ALBANS,** *Ye Old Fighting Cocks 1921* 70484

Although the Fighting Cocks appears to be a small octagonal timber-framed building, the undercroft consists of carefully cut blocks of stone standing on massive foundations. The walls of the cellars are lined with flints interspaced with Roman tiles robbed from the nearby town of Verulamium. Before being used as an inn (said to be one of the earliest in the country), it seems that it may have been used as a fishing equipment store by the monastic community at the abbey. The Fighting Cocks stands next to what is thought to have been the abbey fishponds, and the cellars, which lay below the water table, were liable to flooding.

61

FROGMORE, *Holy Trinity Church, Frogmore c1955*
F57006

Frogmore lies about three miles south of St Albans. Built in 1842
to an early design by Giles Gilbert Scott, Holy Trinity was expected
to replace St Peter's parish church. However, shortly after it was
completed, the decision taken in 1840 was reversed. It remained a
chapelry until the amalgamation of the three hamlets of Frogmore,
Park Street and Colney Street into the Parish of Holy Trinity, Frogmore
in 1859. There is no burial ground to the church, as at the time of its
construction the water table was only three feet below the surface.

ST ALBANS, *Market Place c1950* S2075

With not a moving vehicle in view, it would seem that Maypole
Corner in the Market Place had been totally pedestrianised; but
this was a familiar sight on market days. On the right is Maypole,
a branch of the successful grocery shops, forerunners of modern
supermarket chains. Next door is Hancocks, and then a barber's shop
sprouting the familiar red and white poles. The gentleman escorting
the dark-jacketed lady across the road wears a 'demob' suit, part of
a set of clothing given (in a cardboard travelling case) to servicemen
when they were demobilised after the Second World War.

ST ALBANS
The River Ver
1921 70485

The river has been called the Ver from ancient times. Indeed, the Romans named their town Verulamium after the river. In the 1920s this peaceful path was a popular Sunday afternoon stroll, and you would expect to meet only a few people. Today, the riverbank is a bustle of children swishing their sticks in the water and clamouring to buy ice creams from the vendors parked nearby. Nonetheless, the ducks and moorhens manage to thrive on the opposite bank, and the occasional water vole is glimpsed sliding silently into the stream.

ST ALBANS, *Sopwell Nunnery, Lee Hall 1921* 70482

It is said that the original Benedictine nunnery, built on this spot
about half a mile south west of the abbey, was a wooden hut
erected by two devout women who wished to follow a religious
life. When the stone convent was built, the number of nuns
was restricted to thirteen, the two original ladies and eleven
others. Thirteen was considered a fortunate number, as this
reflected Christ and the twelve apostles. When the nunnery was
demolished in the 1530s, Sir Richard Lee managed to save much
of the building, and it was reconstructed in part as Lee Hall.

ST ALBANS
Chequer Street 1921
70481

Chequer Street runs north/ south through the centre of St Albans. To the south it becomes Holywell Hill, and to the north St Peter's Street. The closeness of the market ensured that many of the buildings were places of refreshment - we can see (left) the Bell Hotel, the Bat and Ball, and the Queen's Hotel, where the author Charles Dickens stayed. The flight of Bill Sykes in his book 'Oliver Twist' is peppered with references to Hertfordshire, and on his way back to London, he travelled the road between Hatfield and St Albans. Maybe Dickens had the Queen's Hotel in mind when he wrote the passage. A few hundred yards away, in Catherine Street, stands Bleak House. However, it was given this name in the late 1800s, well after the publication of the book by Charles Dickens of the same name.

▼ ST ALBANS, *French Row 1921* 70478

Running parallel to the Market Place, French Row was little more than an alleyway or service road to the market, overlooked by the clock tower on the left. Around 1747, Dr Joshua Webster wrote: 'The Town of St Albans is ... capable as being laid as dry and clean as any town in the Kingdom, but by bad management is a very Dirty one in Winter ... There is a good Market for Provisions.' Clearly, things had changed by 1921, and it would be difficult to find a tidier and cleaner back road in a market town.

► **ST ALBANS**, *Holywell Hill 1921* 70480

The eastern side of Holywell Hill is peppered with interesting buildings. G W French (left), fruiterer and confectioner, proudly informs the public that he has Lyons tea on sale. Next door is the fine White Hart Hotel; in 1815, the St Albans historian tells us that it was very suitable for 'families and post coaches'. The White Hart had a chequered career. The Scottish Jacobite rebel Lord Lovat stopped here on his way to his execution in London. He had taken a prominent part in Bonnie Prince Charlie's rebellion of 1745, and although aged about 80, he paid the ultimate price. Whilst at the White Hart, William Hogarth painted the last portrait of Lord Lovat.

▶ **ST ALBANS,** *The Abbey Gateway*
1921 70470

The gateway was built in 1362. In 1381,
the peasants' uprising, led by William
Grindcobbe and William Caddington, drew
many rebels from the St Albans area. They
marched to London and were promised
that reforms would take place and that their
grievances would be considered. However,
the mob from St Albans decided not to wait
and set about enforcing their demands.
They caused considerable damage in the
town, and then turned their attention on
the abbey. They confronted Abbot Thomas
de la Mere, who firmly shut the gate in their
faces; but the mob were not to be put off, and
eventually the abbot opened the gate. The
rebels burnt many of the old charters and
documents, and ripped up the millstones in
the floor of the parlour.

◀ **ST ALBANS**
*St Peter's Street
1921* 70472

The baker's and Cornwell's Tea Rooms on the right are about to receive their daily delivery of milk from the horse-drawn milk float hiding behind the tree. Passing by is a particularly fine, and almost new, Vauxhall four-seater tourer. In the background is the pillared portico of the Town Hall, which had been opened in 1831. It was in St Peter's Street, close to its junction with Victoria Street (the turning in the left distance), that the leader of the Lancastrians, Edward Beaufort, Duke of Somerset was killed in May 1455 during the Wars of the Roses.

▼ **ST ALBANS,** *The Abbey from the North 1886* 19453

King Offa of Mercia built a small wooden church on the site of the present abbey. It has grown into an impressive edifice, much of which is constructed of bricks and stone rescued from the nearby Roman town of Verulamium. It is believed that in the early 4th century, Alban, a Christian martyr, was beaten to death on the hill opposite the town and then beheaded. Offa found the bones of St Alban, and in AD793 built the abbey church. It was rebuilt shortly after the Norman Conquest, and then purchased by the people of St Albans after the Dissolution of the Monasteries.

▶ **HEMEL HEMPSTEAD**
The Marlowes c1960 H255007

The new town of Hemel Hempstead was built in the expectation that it would be 'catering for all needs.' The new Marlowes, the main shopping centre, bore little visible relation to the original street with its Victorian, and earlier, jumble of shops, pubs and businesses. These were demolished to make way for this wide boulevard. The shops reflected a new affluence and modern needs. In the distance stand the post office and the gas and electricity showrooms; just visible is the pedestrian foot bridge to assist shoppers to cross the road. Construction work is still under way.

▼ **HEMEL HEMPSTEAD,** *St Mary's Church c1955* H255008

St Mary's Church dates from around 1150, and is considered to be one of the finest churches of its style in Hertfordshire. The 14th-century spire was originally clad in wooden shingles, but was later covered with fluted lead. One of the peal of eight bells dates from 1604, and is endorsed 'God Save King James'. Soon after the photograph was taken, the iron railings were removed and replaced with a low wall.

▶ **BERKHAMSTED,** *The Old Court House c1960* B407046

One of the oldest buildings in Berkhamsted, the half-timbered Court House dates
from the Tudor period. It was founded as the town's first 'civic centre' under a
charter of King James I dated 18 July 1618. In 1860, Lord Brownlow of Ashridge
took the Court House as part of the Manor of Berkhamsted; he paid £43,682. It was
then leased to a group of trustees at a peppercorn rent and continued as a National
School. It later became the home of the verger of St Peter's Church.

BERKHAMSTED, *The Grand Union Canal c1960* B407049

The Grand Union Canal Company was formed by a merger of the Regent's
Canal & Dock Co in London with the Grand Junction Canal, amongst
others, in 1923. It was an attempt to combat increasing competition
with road and rail transport. The steam-powered narrow boats were
replaced with diesel-powered vessels, and by the late 1930s very few of
the originals survived. Despite a number of initiatives, including the
widening of all the bridges to Birmingham, the decline was irreversible.
Eventually, in 1968 the canal was designated a 'recreational waterway';
although attempts were made to revive its commercial operation, its
future appears to be as a leisure facility.

▲ **TRING,** *Tring Park 1897* 39647

This house is said to have been given to Nell Gwynn by King Charles II, although there is no positive evidence. Nonetheless, what is certain is that the king often visited Henry Guy, the owner, when Nell was also being entertained there. The building in the photograph bears little resemblance to the original, although the reconstruction of 1874-75 used the Wren structure at its core. In the later 1800s and early 1900s, kangaroos, emus, zebra, wild horses, tortoises and cranes wandered freely on these lawns and flower beds in front of the south (rear) facade.

◄ **TRING,** *New Mill c1955*
N153006

The Queens Arms stands at the crossroads of the Upper Icknield Way and the road between Tring and Long Marston. Ford Road falls away in front of the camera and leads down to the crossing over the Grand Union Canal and thence to the reservoirs at Tringford. The dockside at New Mills Wharf was once the site of a successful narrow boat building industry until the early 1900s, but the arrival of road transport spelt the end of the trade. New Mill saw the start of the religious sect known as the Particular Baptists around 1689. From here, the denomination spread, and Particular Baptist chapels were to be found all over England by the mid 1800s.

HARPENDEN, *High Street c1960* H25032

The Frith photographer stands opposite Station Road and looks north along the High Street. Harpenden Central railway station, in Station Road, serves passengers for London and Bedford and those wishing to ride on the 'Nickey Line'. Originally, the High Street was bordered with even more trees, but many were removed in 1935 as they were considered a hazard to traffic; later, many fell victim to disease. Hidden behind the trees on the left stands the George Hotel, always a popular stopping place for travellers.

HARPENDEN, *High Street c1960* H25061

The White Lion, in the centre of the buildings on the right, was built in 1890 on the site of a large house and walled garden. It originally sported a very fine white stone lion mounted above the door. Sad to say, the bracket failed to support it, and the lion was removed. A row of Victorian shops (Gibson, estate agents; Herbert Irons, undertaker; and Levi Witcham, tobacconist) and dwellings was demolished in 1936, and the modern building past the White Horse was erected. The High Road was heavily used by horse-drawn traffic; even in 1910, the town council employed a full-time horse manure collector to keep the road clear. Most of the trees were cut down in 1935, and the remainder were lost through Dutch elm disease in the early 1980s.

KIMPTON, *High Street 1965*
K94009

Kimpton lies midway between Hitchin and St Albans. It is mentioned in the Domesday Book as having woodland for 800 pigs. This represents a huge area of oak woods kept under control by the animals to provide timber for building. The white house (left) is probably one of the oldest in the village and has a timber frame. On the oak beam over the porch are carved the initials CC, those of Charles Chalkley, whose family owned the property from 1590 until 1960, when it was sold and converted into an antiques shop. In the old days, the High Street was liable to flooding; occasionally in recent years the villagers have blocked their doors with sandbags.

WHITWELL, *High Street 1952* W175003

On the right is the Swan pub, whilst further down on the left stands the Bull, dating from the 1600s. In their book 'Haunted Hertfordshire', Ruth Stratton and Nicholas Connell tell us about a Napoleonic recruiting sergeant who appeared to tempt the customers at the Bull. During building work in the 1930s, a skeleton dressed in the shreds of a uniform were uncovered and given a Christian burial. The ghost was never seen again! It is also said that every Tuesday the spirit of Betty Deacon fries her sprats at the top of Bury Hill, Whitwell. It seems that 'the other world' can be recognised not only by sight and sound, but also by smell.

HITCHIN
Sun Street 1901
46635

Sun Street takes its name from the Sun Hotel (centre right). It is said that the first public coach in Hitchin belonged to the landlord. In 1772, three highwaymen robbed a coach at the Sun; their initials, and the date, can still be seen carved into the bricks above the door arch. The coaching trade came to an end around 1850 when the railway arrived. Colonel Somerset attempted to revive the coach route between the Sun and the George at Enfield using his delightfully named four-in-hand the 'Hirondelle'.

HITCHIN, *William Ransom Buildings, Bancroft 1931* 84206

William Ransom, a Quaker, was born in Bancroft in the mid 1820s. He was educated at Isaac Brown's Academy and was a contemporary of Joseph Lister the physician, Birket Foster the watercolourist, and Joseph Pollard the botanist. Ransom was apprenticed to Southalls, manufacturing chemists, of Birmingham, and later used his skills to set up the pharmaceutical company that still bears his name. Amongst the company's activities was the growing of lavender, which was originally used in medical preparations and later in the production of toilet water and perfumes. This view shows the entrance to W Ransom & Sons' yard in 1931.

HITCHIN, *Market Place c1940* H89026

This view was probably photographed in the late 1930s, for not one car
here dates from the post-war period. The AA-badged Vauxhall 14, the
Morris 8 Series II, the Ford Y Model, the Morris Z-Type van, the Ford
E83W van and the large American car (is it a Chrysler?) were all built
in the 1930s. Even the telephone box is of the late pre-war 'concrete'
period rather than the traditional post office red cast-iron type. In the
background, the excellent Hitchin Museum tells us that Maison Gerrard
(left) replaced Waldock's 'Feather Dresser, Wool & Fancy Repository' of
the early 1900s, and Myers (far left) replaced Mrs Elizabeth Maria Budd,
'Suppliers of Hercules Boots' in the late 1890s.

UP THE A1

ELSTREE, *The Village c1955* E103016a

The gabled building in the far distance formed part of the original St Nicholas's Church of England School, built in 1884. Elstree Stores and Post Office (right) was demolished in the early 1980s as almost the final part of the huge redevelopment of the village. The post office had a chequered career; at one time, it occupied part of Manaton House on the right. The six bells in St Nicholas's church were recast in 1879 by John Warner, whose brother Septimus built the Italian Cottage, later known as the Spinning Wheel, at Hoddesdon (see page 32).

ELSTREE, *High Street c1955* E103016b

The name Elstree is a complicated derivative of 'High Street': Heaghstre in Anglo-Saxon times, through Ilestree to the modern Elstree. You would be forgiven for thinking that this was a row of Tudor houses. It is, in fact, a relatively modern frontage on a group of late 18th-century timber-framed buildings. The premises closest to the photographer were occupied by Barclays Bank. Like so much of Elstree, the buildings were destroyed during the 'improvements' to the High Street of the 1960s and 70s and replaced with a block of maisonettes.

▶ **BOREHAMWOOD**
The Church of St Michael and All Angels c1965 B408035

The foundation stone was laid in October 1954 by the late Princess Margaret and blessed by the Lord Bishop of St Albans. St Michael's was built to provide a church for the rapidly expanding town of Borehamwood. The bell came from the mortuary chapel at Ayot St Peter, and had been donated by Charles Willes Wilshere of The Frythe in 1876. Did the Frith photographer realise the family connection?

▼ **SOUTH MIMMS,** *St Giles's Church 1966* S829017

It was only in the year before this photograph was taken that South Mimms became part of Hertfordshire - the parish had previously formed part of Middlesex, and was forgotten even by the Domesday Survey. The tranquillity of St Giles's (a dedication unknown until Norman times) was soon to be shattered when the junction of the M25 and A1 was built close by. Pevsner says of the Frowyk memorial in the church: 'A remarkable example of the gusto with which craftsmen at some distance to the Court threw themselves into the new Italian fashion.' The exterior, however, shows no sign of the 'remarkable' interior – it is just a fine flint-faced building dating from the 13th century and, like so many others, rebuilt in the 1870s.

► **COLNEY STREET,** *Old Moor Mill c1955*
C759008

Today, the ford and bridge have disappeared and the mill nestles under the southern carriageway of the M25. In the 1950s and 60s, the mill (on Smug Oak Lane) was a well-known television star, frequently used by the production companies working at Elstree and Borehamwood. It appears in H G Wells's 'Invisible Man', 'The Avengers', 'Danger Man', and 'The Baron,' but its starring role was in three episodes of 'The Saint'. In 'The Chequered Flag' (1965), Simon Templar, played by Roger Moore, drives Catherine Marshall (played by Pamela Conway) in his famous Volvo P1800 sports car. The second episode was 'The Fiction Maker' (1966), when Simon Templar crosses the bridge towards Smug Oak. Finally, it appears in 'Legacy for the Saint' (1968), where, again, the Volvo races across the bridge.

◄ **HATFIELD**
The Eight Bells
c1960 H254046

It was at the Eight Bells (then known as the Five Bells) at the corner of Park Street and Fore Street that Charles Dickens is said to have stayed when he was sent, as a young reporter, to Hatfield to write about the death in a fire of the first Marchioness of Salisbury. When he later wrote 'Oliver Twist', he had Bill Sykes stop for refreshment here after he had murdered Nancy.

► **HATFIELD**
Church Cottage
c1955 H245006

Church Cottage has traditionally been the residence of the senior curate to Hatfield parish church since 1920. The building was carefully restored by F W Speight, a local antiques dealer, between 1910 and 1930. He renovated a number of buildings in old Hatfield, and the value of his work has not been fully recognised. However, it should be remembered that many of the features and the contents of the houses were not originally from Hatfield. He was very happy to import any items that he felt were needed to complement a building!

◄ **HATFIELD**
The Technical College
c1965 H254073

Hatfield Technical College was founded in 1951. This campus was built by Hertfordshire County Council on a site at Roe Green given by de Havilland, the aircraft manufacturer. It changed its name to Hatfield College of Technology in 1958, and became Hatfield Polytechnic College in 1968. In more recent years it has been part of the University of Hertfordshire.

▲ **HATFIELD,** *St Albans Road c1955* H254008

Threatened with closure in 1930 but reprieved, the White Lion (right) underwent a major rebuild in 1935. It remained open during the work, and the family proudly continued to serve their customers. However, in the early 1960s, when owned by Benskins, it was demolished to make way for an office block and dwellings. Later, the offices' car park was pedestrianised. The light grey building on the right with the twin chimney pots is the Boar and Castle, owned by the brewers J W Green. When it closed in 1964, it belonged to Whitbreads. Motoring historians will be pleased to see the Morris 10/4 (or is it a rare 25?) parked just past the White Lion.

◄ **HATFIELD,** *The Market Place c1965* H254053

When the new town was built in the 1960s, this part of the development was a busy and thriving out-door market. One of the more popular stalls, located close to the tree in the right foreground, sold off-cuts of wood, and many newly married couples fitted out their homes in the new town with shelves and furniture made from surplus timber. The strange octagonal kiosk on the right was the market manager's office. It did not last long, and was soon demolished. The so-called Balcony Shops were: the Continental, men's hair stylist; Universal Music Co; the Olympic Restaurant; Stewart Cameras; Billing & Howard, ironmongers; R W Bradshaw, Hatfield Eye Centre; Mandan Toys; the Beauty Centre; and A Gould.

HATFIELD, *The Salisbury Hotel c1955* H254301

It is also claimed that Charles Dickens stayed at the Salisbury Hotel when he visited Hatfield. Lord Byron's body rested here on its way to burial at Newstead Abbey, and his mistress Lady Caroline Lamb is buried with her husband, Lord Melbourne, at St Etheldreda's church opposite. Lord Melbourne is not the only prime minister buried at Hatfield - not far away, in the same churchyard, lie the remains of Robert Cecil, third Marquis of Salisbury.

HATFIELD, *St Etheldreda's c1965* H254082

The parish church was built during the reign of Henry III and heavily restored in 1871. A spire was added in 1846 to commemorate the visit of Queen Victoria to the town, but it was removed in 1930. It was found that iron nails (instead of copper) and sawn shingles (in place of cleft shingles) had been used in its construction. The interior is studded with memorials and monuments to the Cecils/Salisburys, who have their own burial ground guarded by a set of iron gates from St Paul's churchyard.

▼ **HATFIELD,** *The de Havilland Factory, the New Design Block c1955* H254077

The first aircraft built by Geoffrey de Havilland was constructed 1909 in a small workshop in Fulham. It flew for a few yards at Seven Barrows in Hampshire and then crashed, leaving only the propeller and engine worth saving. However, de Havilland persevered, and in 1920 opened a factory at Stag Lane in Edgware. When war with Germany became a possibility, a new headquarters was built at Hatfield for the de Havilland Aircraft Company; it became a division of Hawker Siddely Aviation in 1959. Sir Geoffrey (he had been knighted in 1944) died in May 1965, and shortly afterwards the factory was closed. The remaining part of the company was absorbed into British Aerospace in 1977.

► **WELWYN**
The Clock Restaurant c1955
W293002

When motoring became popular in the 1920s, many 'road houses' were built to cater for the needs of travellers. The Clock Restaurant is a typical example; close to the A1 at Welwyn, it is a well-known meeting place for businessmen and tourists. It has changed little since this photograph was taken, and even today is instantly recognisable from the motorway.

◄ **HATFIELD,** *Hatfield House c1965* H254062

In 1607, King James I exchanged the Manor of Hatfield for Theobalds, near Cheshunt (later the home of Lord and Lady Meux and Temple Bar), which was owned by Sir Robert Cecil. Work on the new building was begun soon after. The main frontage is about 280 feet long, and the wings about 100 feet deep; the cost of the main building was £9,209. The architect was either John of Padua or Bernard Jensen. Princess Elizabeth was imprisoned at Hatfield House, and the oak tree still stands in the park where, it is said, she was sitting when told of her sister Queen Mary's death and her accession to the throne as Elizabeth I. When Queen Victoria visited Hatfield in 1846 she collected an acorn from the tree to plant it at Windsor. It is believed that from that day, the oak 'shed no more acorns.'

► **WELWYN,** *High Street c1955* W293006

In his excellent history of the town, Tony Rook tells us that Welwyn only began to become a substantial settlement in the 17th century. Of course, by then the parish church of St Mary the Virgin was well established; parts of it, like St Albans Abbey, were built from the remains of a nearby Roman settlement. It was almost totally rebuilt in 1911 and again in 1952 when a fire damaged the east end.

WELWYN
Church Street c1955
W293008

Church Street runs north-eastwards from the High Street towards the new town of Welwyn Garden City. On the right is the local branch of Barclays Bank, and further down, next to the parked Morris van, stands Holly Hall. Three young women, dressed in the height of 1950s fashion, pass the white L-plated Bedford van, whilst the smart young men on the other side walk past the totally obscured Church House.

WELWYN, *Church Street c1955* W293009

Further down Church Street, we can see (left) white Church House, an early Georgian building, now a private residence but once the police station. Just past the motorcycle parked outside J C Johnson's shop is the Rose and Crown pub. This is first mentioned in 1633; it may have originally been known as the Rose. Behind the Rose and Crown, in Anchor Pightle, was the playground to the school opened in 1739 by Dr Young. Another earlier school had operated from Church House in 1714. When school provision became more formalised, one of the assistants at the Ivy School was Miss Ann Van Gogh, who was on at least one occasion visited by her brother, Vincent, the famous artist.

WELWYN, *Danesbury Hospital c1960* W293031

The original Danesbury was almost totally destroyed by fire in September 1920 when the Welwyn Fire Brigade's manual pumps were unable to halt the spread of the flames. (It is interesting to note that one of the earliest fire and rescue facilities in Welwyn hung under the eaves of the jetty of Church House: this was a long pole with an iron hook used to drag the thatch off the roofs of burning buildings). In 1922, Danesbury was bought by Middlesex County Council for use as a hospital for convalescents and later the incurably ill. It continued until 1994, when the New Danesbury hospital was built next to Queen Victoria Hospital.

WELWYN GARDEN CITY, *The Fountain, Parkway c1955* W294011

In 1888, Ebenezer Howard read 'Looking Backward': a sleeper awakens in AD 2000, when America is run on a co-operative and community basis. This fired his imagination, and he developed the concept of Garden Cities. The first to be built was Letchworth, and in 1919 the proposal to build the second near Welwyn gained general approval. George Bernard Shaw, who lived at nearby Ayot St Lawrence, described Howard as 'an elderly nobody' yet 'an amazing man'. This fountain epitomises the green open spaces in which Howard delighted, and stands as a memorial to his foresight.

WELWYN GARDEN CITY, *Welwyn Department Stores c1955*
W294020

Designed by de Soissons, Welwyn Department Stores opened in June 1939 and operated as part of the Howardsgate Investment Trust. As well as the shopping area (now a branch of John Lewis), there were 62 residential flats and a Masonic suite. The local council later used part of the store as a depot, and this was demolished about ten years after this photograph was taken to form Rosanne House.

◄ **WELWYN GARDEN CITY,** *Station Approach c1955* W294045

The first true railway station was built here in October 1920, the butt of many jokes, as it was some distance from the town across muddy fields and bumpy building sites. A new station was opened in October 1926 whose design could not be more of a contrast. The first station had a single draughty open platform with a small shed-like waiting room. The new station was a grander affair with a pillared entrance and spacious waiting rooms and booking halls. It was not until the building of the Howard Centre in 1990 that a finer building could be found in the city.

WELWYN GARDEN CITY, *Digswell Corner c1960*
W294118b

Digswell, on the road between Old Welwyn, Welwyn Garden City and Hertford, has changed little over the years, and its position overlooking the Mimram Valley must have been familiar to generations of Hertfordshire people. For well over a hundred years, however, the valley has been spanned by the giant railway viaduct 100 feet high and 1490 feet long. Nothing, however magnificent, has been allowed to damage this tranquil spot.

WELWYN GARDEN CITY, *The Cherry Tree c1960*
W294056

Unlike Letchworth, Welwyn Garden City was not to be 'dry.' When Letchworth was built, there were no pubs; but it was agreed that the construction workers at Welwyn needed a 'wet canteen', and so the Cherry Tree was built. Originally it was a wooden building, 'primitive and pioneer', and run by the Welwyn Restaurant Company. In 1932 it was decided that the Cherry Tree should be modernised; Whitbreads won the contract, and designed by R G Muir, the new Cherry Tree was opened early in 1933. It was transformed into a Waitrose supermarket in 1991, and the bowling green at the back was converted into a car park.

► **CODICOTE**
*The George &
Dragon c1960*
C320025

While the gentry
stayed at the George
and Dragon Inn, their
retainers would have
lodged at the Goat
next door, close to the
site of what was the
Tabard, or even in the
hayloft of the barn
behind. The George
and Dragon was later
renamed As You Like
It! The shops on the
left were built on the
site of the farm and
yard owned since the
1700s by the Fisher
family. Further down
is Codicote Motors,
originally Porter's
Garage, later owned by
J Robarts & Sons.

► **CODICOTE,** *High Street c1960*
C320038

Between the telephone kiosk and
the pretty two-tone Austin A series
car stands the Globe public house
(centre right). Known to the local
people as 'Help me through the
World' (the sign showed a human
figure bursting through the top of
the globe), it was kept in the late
1800s and early 1900s by the Males
family, who ran a builder's and
decorator's business for many years.
Strong ale known as 'Crackskull' was
sold here - inevitably the landlord
was called 'Cracky' Males. In 1944,
a flying bomb skimmed over the
High Street and landed at Codicote
Bottom, causing considerable
damage to the houses there.

▼ CODICOTE, *St Giles's Church c1960* C320040

Dedicated to St Giles, the patron saint of beggars, cripples, hunters and travellers, the parish church contains the Chapel of the Holy Innocents. It was consecrated about 1110 by Ralph, Bishop of Rochester, but little of the original structure survived the regular renovations culminating in the major restoration of 1853. A short walk away lies the hamlet of Hogsnorton. In the 1940s/50s, when Gillie Potter broadcast his popular series of village tales under that name, the villagers realised that he did not know that a real Hogsnorton existed. They invited him to visit, and he became a firm friend of the community.

► KNEBWORTH, *London Road 1965* K43027

The modern village of Knebworth stands astride the main London to Stevenage railway line. The original community, which served the Knebworth estate, lay about 1½ miles to the west at what is now Old Knebworth; but when the railway arrived in the 1850, a new complex of housing, businesses and shops developed to the east and west of the London/Stevenage roads and the railway. The photograph shows the southern end of the village, with Barclays Bank on the right and the empty Morris showroom on the left.

97

KNEBWORTH, *Knebworth House 1901* 46662

Knebworth appears in Domesday as 'Cheneepeworde'. Knebworth
House was originally built by Sir Robert Lytton in the 16th century.
In 1811 much of the old building was pulled down, and the surviving
west wing was enriched with battlements, panelled turrets crowned
with copper domes, dragons on pinnacles, and faces and gargoyles
sprouting everywhere. The Lytton family still live at Knebworth House,
but the gardens (near the busy A1 motorway) are now open to the
public. At weekends, the 260-acre park rings to the modern sounds of
pop concerts, classic car rallies, and the hiss of hot air balloons.

STEVENAGE, *The Ruins of St Etheldreda's Church, Chesfield 1899* 44280

The village of Chesfield lay about a mile north of Stevenage close to Graveley. The church had been built some time before 1291. When the Black Death struck Hertfordshire, Chesfield was one of the many villages which were abandoned. Although the village had almost disappeared, services continued until 1731; the last marriage took place here in January 1728, and the last burial was that of the Vicar of Pirton in March 1731. Demolition was sanctioned by the Bishop of Lincoln in 1750, and it is said that some of the material was used to restore Graveley church. The ruins of St Etheldreda's still exist, but time and ivy have taken their toll - the photograph shows much more of the structure than survives today.

STEVENAGE, *High Street and the Bowling Green 1901* 46509

Now fenced off and part of a busy road complex, the triangular Bowling
Green in the distance became the site of the town's war memorial. On
the right, the house with the pillared portico (the pillars are said to have
come from St Nicholas's church) is The Grange, previously the Swan Inn.
In the 1600s and 1700s the Swan was only rivalled in importance by the
White Lion, both on the busy Great North Road. During the Great War,
the Grange was used as a work station manufacturing field dressings and
bandages, whilst during the Second World War it was used by the County
Council to house lads who had been evacuated from London.

STEVENAGE, *The Post Office and the White Lion 1901* 46512

The post office, demonstrating the town's civic and patriotic pride, was built in 1887, but it later moved to new premises next to the Yorkshire Grey in 1913. Further down stands the White Lion (with the light wall). In the 1770s, it owned about 30 acres, and also numerous barns and outbuildings. These came in useful during the Napoleonic Wars, when French prisoners of war were housed there during their journey north to the camp at Yaxley near Peterborough. Unfortunately, the gateway to the White Lion was too low for coaches and passengers, and horses had to be changed on the hard standing in front of the inn.

STEVENAGE
*The High Street
looking North 1903*
49769

In the distance are the houses facing the Bowling Green. On the left is the White Lion, looking over the wide street which was used for the cattle and general market. The ponds behind the inn were used to refresh the animals, whilst the White Lion served the same need to the drivers and farmers. The market finally closed in the 1960s when the last of the traders moved their stalls to the open-air market in the new town centre. At the north-east corner of the White Lion, on its brick pillar and protected by a wooden gable, is the bell, erected in 1887, used to call the finely liveried Stevenage Town Fire Brigade.

STEVENAGE, *Rockingham Way c1955* S191036

This photograph typifies the new town. In 1947, after much
opposition from the locals, the Stevenage New Town Act was
passed and the Stevenage Development Corporation was formed.
There was an influx of newcomers from London, and many
locals were confused by their different accents and ways. More
cars appeared, and modern shops, topped in this case by living
accommodation, served each community of 10,000 people. It
seems that traffic regulations were not strongly enforced - the
Morris 'Z' type van is parked across the corner of the junction,
the Austin 10 stands well out from the kerb, and the Ford Popular
blocks the entrance to the service bay. Only the elderly Morris 8
series 1 appears to be observing the Highway Code!

STEVENAGE, *Norton Green c1940* S191015

Norton Green lies to the west of Stevenage and the A1 road. In her
'History & Guide to Stevenage', Margaret Ashby tells us the story of
Annie Sharp of Norton Green, who in 1882 was sent home by public
transport suffering from a fever - the family at Hitchin did not want
her in their home when they realised that it might be potentially fatal
scarlet fever. Indeed, Dr Hill Smith diagnosed that this was exactly
what was wrong with her, and she was sent away from her parents
and five brothers and sisters to the Stevenage Cottage Hospital.
Annie survived, and the editor of the Stevenage Parish Magazine
reported: 'We do not know whether this is a case of ignorance or of
reckless and selfish carelessness; but we know the wonder is that in
the face of such facts infectious diseases do not spread.'

STEVENAGE, *St George's Church c1960* S191099

As befitted a new town, the church of St George on the corner of
St George's Way and Cutty's Lane was built to a forward-thinking
design in 1956. When the church was completed, the sunlight
burst through the vast windows, creating a beacon which could
be seen from miles around. Unfortunately, the planners did not
appreciate the aesthetic importance of natural illumination:
shortly after St George's dedication, a tall, dark office block
was built to the right. Although its architecture faced some
opposition, today the church personifies the optimistic outlook
of the community. The fine town museum in the undercroft looks
back at the historical heritage of the villages and greens that
make up the old and new towns of Stevenage.

STEVENAGE, *Broomin Green Farm c1955* S191003

The new town of Stevenage was built over a matrix of villages and greens. One of the sad losses was the destruction of the community at Broomin Green at the southern end of what is now Fairview Avenue. In her book on the history of Stevenage, Margaret Ashby tells us that it was on the level crossing close to Broomin Green that two children walking to school from Norton Green were killed by an express train in thick fog. On a happier note, this farmhouse survives today - so many early buildings were destroyed. It stands as a reminder of what we have lost in the name of progress.

WALKERN, *The White Lion c1960* W289004

The White Lion lies on the main road through the village. The road meanders through the countryside from Hertford and Stevenage through Walkern to Cromer and Cottered. During the 1800s, both side of the High Street were dotted with inns and public houses; even today, three or four survive. Little has changed in the years since this photograph was taken, save for the building of a service station and a new village shop. Travellers from the turn of the century would still recognise Walkern.

BALDOCK, *White Horse Street c1955* B9015

It is amazing to realise that at the time of writing, a new by-pass is being built to avoid the cross-roads at White Horse Street/High Street. The only moving car in sight here is in the far distance, whilst five cars, including an Austin 10 and a Morris 8 Series 2 convertible, are standing in what is now a very busy parking bay. It hardly seem necessary to have a 'Slow' sign on the road - even today, the nose-to-tail traffic moves at little more than a snail's pace.

BALDOCK, *White Horse Street c1960* B9030

It is about five years after B9015 was taken (previous page), and this time we are looking eastwards towards Royston. There is still only a couple of cars driving on the road, with absolutely no suggestion of the congestion of forty years later. And still there is a 'Slow' sign painted on the tarmac! Only the more modern cars give us the clue to the slightly later date.

LETCHWORTH, *Leys Avenue 1908* 60885

Well before the completion of the construction of the Garden
City, Boots (right) had established themselves in Leys Avenue
between the Wynd and Norton Way South. The road curves
off westwards towards the site of the temporary wooden GNR
railway station. Even at this late date, the town omnibus was
horse-drawn (providing a link to the 'permanent' Hitchin railway
station) and, indeed, a motor bus service did not begin until
1920.

LETCHWORTH
Leys Avenue c1927
71903

Although Ebenezer Howard had hoped to create a single shopping centre in Letchworth, retailers took individual leases on the shops. There was an intentional lack of continuity in the design of the shops on the south (left) side of the avenue. Bennet and Bidwell were commissioned to ensure there would be variety in their style so as to produce a 'village feel' to the parade. Motor enthusiasts will be pleased to note the superb Buick preparing to demolish the cyclist!

LETCHWORTH, *Norton Way 1922* 71906

The owner of the Ford Model T proudly drives his vehicle along Norton Way. The car was probably built in the assembly plant in Manchester.

LETCHWORTH, *Baldock Road 1922* 71908

Little has changed along Baldock Road over the years. The trees
still overhang the road, and the little lodge survives charmingly
intact. Only the traffic is heavier and the roadside spoiled by
direction and traffic control signs. But do not be deceived:
now lurking among the foliage of the trees and bushes are the
ubiquitous speed cameras, waiting to catch the unwary motorist
whose attention has been diverted by the pretty hedgerows.

NORTON, *The Village c1955* N196015

The village of Norton was clearly one of the Frith company's favourite locations in Hertfordshire, for this view was taken time after time at almost ten-year intervals. A moving film of its development could easily be made into a 'flicker-book'. Little has changed since the 1950s. A new picket fence has been erected round the large house on the right, and the Three Horseshoes now sports a new illuminated sign. The old 'torch' school sign has disappeared, and a bus stop has sprouted in its place (centre left). It seems that local authority budget cuts had bitten hard in the 1950s - the grass verges have not been trimmed, and the road needs repair and resurfacing.

INDEX

FRITH PRODUCTS & SERVICES

Francis Frith would doubtless be pleased to know that the pioneering publishing venture he started in 1860 still continues today. Over a hundred and forty years later, The Francis Frith Collection continues in the same innovative tradition and is now one of the foremost publishers of vintage photographs in the world. Some of the current activities include:

INTERIOR DECORATION

Today Frith's photographs can be seen framed and as giant wall murals in thousands of pubs, restaurants, hotels, banks, retail stores and other public buildings throughout the country. In every case they enhance the unique local atmosphere of the places they depict and provide reminders of gentler days in an increasingly busy and frenetic world.

PRODUCT PROMOTIONS

Frith products are used by many major companies to promote the sales of their own products or to reinforce their own history and heritage. Frith promotions have been used by Hovis bread, Courage beers, Scots Porage Oats, Colman's mustard, Cadbury's foods, Mellow Birds coffee, Dunhill pipe tobacco, Guinness, and Bulmer's Cider.

GENEALOGY AND FAMILY HISTORY

As the interest in family history and roots grows world-wide, more and more people are turning to Frith's photographs of Great Britain for images of the towns, villages and streets where their ancestors lived; and, of course, photographs of the churches and chapels where their ancestors were christened, married and buried are an essential part of every genealogy tree and family album.

FRITH PRODUCTS

All Frith photographs are available Framed or just as Mounted Prints and Posters (size 23 x 16 inches). These may be ordered from the address below. Other products available are - Address Books, Calendars, Jigsaws, Canvas Prints, Postcards and local and prestige books.

THE INTERNET

Already ninety thousand Frith photographs can be viewed and purchased on the internet through the Frith websites and a myriad of partner sites.

For more detailed information on Frith products, look at this site:
www.francisfrith.com

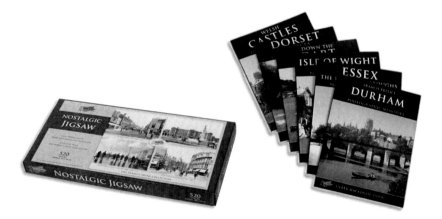

See the complete list of Frith Books at: www.francisfrith.com
This web site is regularly updated with the latest list of publications from The Francis Frith Collection. If you wish to buy books relating to another part of the country that your local bookshop does not stock, you may purchase on-line.

For further information, trade, or author enquiries please contact us at the address below:
The Francis Frith Collection, Unit 6, Oakley Business Park, Wylye Road, Dinton, Wiltshire SP3 5EU.
Tel: +44 (0)1722 716 376 Fax: +44 (0)1722 716 881 Email: sales@francisfrith.co.uk

See Frith products on the internet at www.francisfrith.com

FREE PRINT OF YOUR CHOICE

Mounted Print
Overall size 14 x 11 inches (355 x 280mm)

Choose any Frith photograph in this book.
Simply complete the Voucher opposite and
return it with your remittance for £3.50 (to cover
postage and handling) and we will print the
photograph of your choice in SEPIA (size 11 x 8
inches) and supply it in a cream mount with a
burgundy rule line (overall size 14 x 11 inches).
Please note: aerial photographs and
photographs with a reference number
starting with a "Z" are not Frith photographs
and cannot be supplied under this offer.
Offer valid for delivery to one UK address only.

**PLUS: Order additional Mounted Prints
at HALF PRICE - £9.50 each** (normally £19.00)
If you would like to order more Frith prints from
this book, possibly as gifts for friends and family,
you can buy them at half price (with no
additional postage and handling costs).

PLUS: Have your Mounted Prints framed
For an extra £18.00 per print you can have your
mounted print(s) framed in an elegant polished
wood and gilt moulding, overall size
16 x 13 inches (no additional postage and
handling required).

IMPORTANT!

These special prices are only available if you use
this form to order. You must use the ORIGINAL
VOUCHER on this page (no copies permitted). We
can only despatch to one UK address. This offer
cannot be combined with any other offer.

Send completed Voucher form to:
**The Francis Frith Collection, Unit 6,
Oakley Business Park, Wylye Road,
Dinton, Wiltshire SP3 5EU**

CHOOSE A PHOTOGRAPH FROM THIS BOOK

Voucher for **FREE** and Reduced Price Frith Prints

*Please do not photocopy this voucher. Only the original is valid,
so please fill it in, cut it out and return it to us with your order.*

Picture ref no	Page no	Qty	Mounted @ £9.50	Framed + £18.00	Total Cost £
		1	Free of charge*	£	£
			£9.50	£	£
			£9.50	£	£
			£9.50	£	£
			£9.50	£	£
			£9.50	£	£

Please allow 28 days for delivery. Offer available to one UK address only

* Post & handling		£3.80
Total Order Cost		£

Title of this book . . . .

I enclose a cheque/postal order for £ . . . .

made payable to 'The Francis Frith Collection'

OR please debit my Mastercard / Visa / Maestro card,
details below

Card Number:

Issue No (Maestro only):   Valid from (Maestro):

Card Security Number: Expires:

Signature:

Name Mr/Mrs/Ms ....

Address ....

....

....

.... Postcode ....

Daytime Tel No ....

Email ....

Valid to 31/12/12

Can you help us with information about any of the Frith photographs in this book?

We are gradually compiling an historical record for each of the photographs in the Frith archive. It is always fascinating to find out the names of the people shown in the pictures, as well as insights into the shops, buildings and other features depicted.

If you recognize anyone in the photographs in this book, or if you have information not already included in the author's caption, do let us know. We would love to hear from you, and will try to publish it in future books or articles.

An Invitation from The Francis Frith Collection to Share Your Memories

The 'Share Your Memories' feature of our website allows members of the public to add personal memories relating to the places featured in our photographs, or comment on others already added. Seeing a place from your past can rekindle forgotten or long held memories. Why not visit the website, find photographs of places you know well and add YOUR story for others to read and enjoy? We would love to hear from you!

www.francisfrith.com/memories

Our production team

Frith books are produced by a small dedicated team at offices near Salisbury. Most have worked with the Frith Collection for many years. All have in common one quality: they have a passion for the Frith Collection.

Frith Books and Gifts

We have a wide range of books and gifts available on our website utilising our photographic archive, many of which can be individually personalised.

www.francisfrith.com